Dear Parents,

Welcome to the Scholastic Reader series. We have taken over 80 years of experience with teachers, parents, and children and put it into a program that is designed to match your child's interests and skills.

Level 1—Short sentences and stories made up of words kids can sound out using their phonics skills and words that are important to remember.

Level 2—Longer sentences and stories with words kids need to know and new "big" words that they will want to know.

Level 3—From sentences to paragraphs to longer stories, these books have large "chunks" of text and are made up of a rich vocabulary.

Level 4—First chapter books with more words and fewer pictures.

It is important that children learn to read well enough to succeed in school and beyond. Here are ideas for reading this book with your child:

- Look at the book together. Encourage your child to read the title and make a prediction about the story.
- Read the book together. Encourage your child to sound out words when appropriate. When your child struggles, you can help by providing the word.
- Encourage your child to retell the story. This is a great way to check for comprehension.
- Have your child take the fluency test on the last page to check progress.

Scholastic Readers are designed to support your child's efforts to learn how to read at every age and every stage. Enjoy helping your child learn to read and love to read.

—**Francie Alexander**
Chief Education Officer
Scholastic Education

Ms. Frizzle

Liz

Written by Joanna Cole.

Based on *The Magic School Bus* books written by Joanna Cole and illustrated by Bruce Degen.

The author and editor would like to thank Steve Quinn of the American Natural History Museum, New York City, for his expert advice in preparing this manuscript.

Illustrations by Carolyn Bracken.

ISBN 0-439-56991-5

20 19 18 17 16

10 11 12 13 14/

Designed by Louise Bova & Maria Stasavage

Printed in the U.S.A.   40
First printing, April 2004

chool Bus®
Flies from the Nest

nold   Ralphie   Keesha   Phoebe   Carlos   Tim   Wanda Dorothy Ann

Cartwheel
·B·O·O·K·S·®

SCHOLASTIC INC.

New York   Toronto   London   Auckland   Sydney
Mexico City   New Delhi   Hong Kong   Buenos Aires

It's fun to be in
Ms. Frizzle's class.

Today we are learning about birds.
Keesha and Carlos want to look
at a robin's nest.
But they can't find a picture.

WE SEE ROBINS IN THE SPRING.

I DON'T SEE ANY.

BACK AND FORTH
by D. A.

Robins go south
for the winter.
They fly back
in the spring.
This is called
migration.

The two robins fly
to the town park.
We go there, too.

The bus changes.
It takes us up.
Now we can see eggs in the nest.

Inside the eggs, the babies
get bigger.
Two weeks later,
they break out of the eggs.

The babies are pink and bare.
And they are *hungry*.
The father and mother bring food.

The robins try to feed Carlos, too.
Carlos does not like worms!

We drop Carlos's lunch.
He catches it.

CHEEP! CHEEP! CHEEP!

YUM!

The little birds
grow soft feathers.
These are called "down."

Then they grow
bigger feathers
on their bodies.

Long feathers grow
on their wings.

At last, it's time to fly.
One by one, the
young robins take off!

One baby doesn't want to go.
The mother bird chirps.
The baby bird flies up, up, up!

Now it's Carlos's turn.
The robins chirp at him.

Ms. Frizzle flies right under him.
He lands in the Magic School Nest.

It was a great trip.
Now we wonder where
we'll go next!

Fluency Fun:

The words in each list below end in the same sounds.
Read the words in a list.
Read them again.
Read them faster.
Try to read all 15 words in one minute.

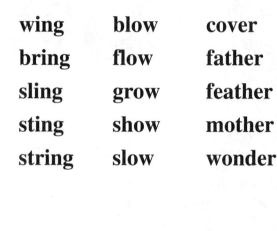

wing	blow	cover
bring	flow	father
sling	grow	feather
sting	show	mother
string	slow	wonder

Look for these words in the story.

bird　**picture**　**climb**

break　**favorite**

Note to Parents:
According to *A Dictionary of Reading and Related Terms,* fluency is "the ability to read smoothly, easily, and readily with freedom from word-recognition problems." Fluency is necessary for good comprehension and enjoyable reading. The activities on this page include a speed drill and a sight-recognition drill. Speed drills build fluency because they help students rapidly recognize common syllables and spelling patterns in words, and they're fun! Sight-recognition drills help students smoothly and accurately recognize words. Practice these activities with your child to help him or her become a fluent reader.

–Wiley Blevins,
Reading Specialist